W9-AHB-707

For: Therese

From: Sister Carleen

Date: Oct 13 - 2000

Illustration Copyright © 1999 Judy Buswell
Text Copyright © 1999

The Brownlow Corporation
6309 Airport Freeway
Fort Worth, Texas 76117

Grateful appreciation is expressed to
Lara Lleverino for her research assistance.

ISBN 1-57051-195-0
Manufactured in China

Friends

Compiled and Written by
Caroline Brownlow

Illustrated by *Judy Buswell*

Little Treasures Miniature Books

Grandmothers Are for Loving

Happiness Is Homemade

Mom, I Love You

My Sister, My Friend

Quiet Moments of Inspiration

Quilted Hearts ✦ Rose Petals

Sisters ✦ Seasons of Friendship

Soft As the Voice of an Angel

Tea Time Friends ✦ They Call It Golf

*How rare and wonderful
is that flash of a moment
when we realize we have
discovered a friend.*

WILLIAM ROTSLER

*Friendship is one of the
sweetest joys of life.
Many might have failed
beneath the bitterness of their trial
had they not found a friend.*

CHARLES H. SPURGEON

*Certain flaws
are necessary for the whole.
It would seem strange
if old friends lacked certain quirks.*

GOETHE

*Dear friends, since God so
loved us, we should love one
another also.*

1 JOHN 4:11

Like the Sunflower

Many flowers open to the sun,
but only one follows him constantly.
Heart, be like the sunflower,
not only open to receive
God's blessings,
but constant in looking to Him.

RICHTER

*Wouldn't it be fun
to live in that town on TV
where the woman always finds
a parking place in front of the bank,
the supermarket and the post office.*

ANONYMOUS

*A friend is one who makes
me do my best.*

OSWALD CHAMBERS

The Birth of Friendship

No birth certificate is issued when
friendship is born. There is nothing
tangible. There is just a feeling that your
life is different and that your
capacity to love and care has miraculously
been enlarged without any effort
on your part. It's like having a tiny
apartment and somebody moves in
with you. But instead of becoming
cramped and crowded,
the space expands, and you discover
rooms you never knew you had
until your friend moved in with you.

STEVE TESICH

A Soul Friend

A soul friend is someone with
whom we can share our greatest joys
and deepest fears,
confess our worst sins and most
persistent faults, clarify our
highest hopes and perhaps most
unarticulated dreams.

EDWARD C. SELLNER

A Friendship Blessing

May the sun always shine
on your windowpane;
May a rainbow be certain
to follow each rain;
May the hand of a friend
always be near you;
May God fill your heart
with gladness to cheer you.

Friendship is a plant
which must often
be watered.

GERMAN PROVERB

Happiness isn't the easiest
thing to find, but one place
you're guaranteed to find
it is in a friend's smile.

ALLISON POLER

*If I had a single flower
for every time I think about you,
I could walk forever in my garden.*

CLAUDIA GRANDI

*A gentleman is a man
who leaves the lawn mower and
garden tools out where
his wife can find them.*

ANONYMOUS

A friend drops their plans
when you're in trouble,
shares joy in your accomplishments,
feels sad when you're in pain.
A friend encourages your dreams
and offers advice—but when you don't
follow it, they still respect
and love you.

DORIS W. HELMERING

If you're going to have friends, you're going to have to be friendly.

PROVERBS 18:24

Judy Buswell
© 1990

*It is hard to believe
that anything is worthwhile,
unless what is infinitely
precious to us is precious
alike to another mind.*

GEORGE ELIOT

Linked by the Heart

Hearts are linked by God.
The friend in whose fidelity you can count,
whose success in life flushes your cheek
with honest satisfaction, whose triumphant
career you have traced and read
with a heart-throbbing almost as if it were
a thing alive, for whose honor you would
answer as for your own; that friend,
given to you by circumstances over which
you have no control, was God's own gift.

F. W. ROBERTSON

A true friend
is someone who thinks
that you are a good egg
even though he knows
that you are slightly cracked.

BERNARD MELTZER

Great Love

*We can do no great things,
only small things with great love.*

MOTHER TERESA

Serve one another in love.

GALATIANS 5:13

The love of our neighbor is the only
door out of the dungeon of self.

GEORGE MACDONALD

A friend is someone who, upon
seeing another friend in immense
pain, would rather be the one
experiencing the pain, than to
have to watch their
friend suffer.

AMANDA GIER

The pleasantness
of one's friend springs
from his earnest counsel.

PROVERBS 27:9

A mere friend will agree with you,

but a real friend will argue.

RUSSIAN PROVERB

We Need Each Other

We are born helpless.
As soon as we are fully conscious
we discover loneliness.
We need others physically,
emotionally, intellectually;
we need them if we are to know
anything, even ourselves.

C. S. LEWIS

A Spiritual Thing

Friendship is a spiritual thing.
It is independent of matter or space
or time. That which I love
in my friend is not that which
I see. What influences me in my
friend is not his body, but his spirit.

JOHN DRUMMOND

One Thing I Give

My friend,
if I could give you one thing,
I would wish for you the ability
to see yourself as others see you.
Then you would realize
what a truly
special person you are.

B. A. BILLINGSLY

A true friend loves
at all times—good and bad.

PROVERBS 17:17

Cosmetics were used in the
Middle Ages; in fact they're
still used in the Middle Ages.

ANONYMOUS

A Friend Is...

A friend is someone who knows the
song in your heart and sings it
back to you when you have
forgotten how it goes.

A friend will know you better in
the first minute they see you than
your acquaintance will
in a thousand years.

A friend is one who believes in you
when you have ceased to believe
in yourself.

A friend is someone who knows you
as you are, understands where you've
been, accepts what you've become
and still gently invites you to grow.

A friend is someone who dances with
you in the sunlight and walks with
you in the shadows.

Coffee, Bears and Friends

Make the attempt if you want to,
but you will find that trying to go
through life without friendship
is like milking a bear to get cream
for your morning coffee.
It is a whole lot of trouble
and then not worth much
after you get it.

ZORA NEALE HURSTON

Think of the number of trees
and blades of grass and flowers,
the extravagant wealth of beauty
no one ever sees!
Think of the sunrises and
sunsets we never look at!
God is lavish in every degree.

OSWALD CHAMBERS

*Real friends
have a great time
doing absolutely
nothing together.*

ANONYMOUS